NORTHUMBERLAND
Loving it!

JIM KEARNEY

HALSGROVE

DEDICATION

I would like to dedicate this book to my sons Ian and Stuart.

ACKNOWLEDGEMENT

I would like to thank my wife Carole for all her help and considerable support not only during the creation of this book but for each and every day.

First published in Great Britain in 2011

If you would like to see more of Jim's work visit his website www.the-image-gallery.com

British Library Cataloguing-in-Publication Data
A CIP record for this title is available from the British Library

ISBN 978 0 85704 037 4

HALSGROVE
Halsgrove House, Ryelands Business Park,
Bagley Road, Wellington, Somerset TA21 9PZ
Tel: 01823 653777 Fax: 01823 216796
email: sales@halsgrove.com

Part of the Halsgrove group of companies.
Information on all Halsgrove titles is
available at: www.halsgrove.com

Printed and bound in China by Everbest Printing Co Ltd

INTRODUCTION

Northumberland, being the least populated county in England offers an abundance of wide open spaces, peace and tranquillity. Having lived all my life in Northumberland, I have spent some considerable time exploring its many delights. In this personal vision of Northumberland I have tried to capture the mood and atmosphere of the natural features of the county.

GEOLOGY

Much of the present day character of Northumberland has been influenced by its geological history. One of the most defining geological events was the creation of the Whin Sill, around 400 million years ago when two tectonic plates collided. The resultant layer of igneous rock was much harder than the surrounding material and over the years much of this material has been eroded to leave spectacular outcrops of the much harder rock exposed.

These outcrops have been utilised over the centuries either as natural defences or as the foundations for many man-made fortifications. A classic example of this is the construction of Hadrian's Wall, which follows the Whin Sill for much of its course. Many of the castles in Northumberland have also utilised this natural foundation and convenient elevation to form the basis of their construction.

THE CASTLES

Northumberland is blessed with some of the most beautiful and historic castles in the world. They stand as a testament to a violent past, whether as a result of skirmishes with the Scots to the north, internal conflicts or the Vikings from the sea. As a consequence of this bloody history, Northumberland has been left with an historical architectural legacy for all to see which ironically seems to instil a sense of peace today.

By choosing to build many of the castles on the Whin Sill, to take advantage of the increased height above the surrounding land, the builders have instinctively followed the natural geological lines in a sympathetic way utilising local materials, which have blended seamlessly to produce castles that almost appear to grow from their surroundings. A perfect example of this is Lindisfarne Castle on Holy Island.

NORTHUMBERLAND NATIONAL PARK

The National Park covers an area of 1048 square kilometres from Hadrian's Wall in the south to the Scottish Border. There is much to see and do within the boundary of the National Park but two of its highlights must be Hadrian's Wall and the Cheviot Hills.

HADRIAN'S WALL

The Roman Emperor Hadrian ordered the construction of the 73-mile wall in AD 122. It is now a World Heritage Site such is its international importance. Much of the wall has long since disappeared, although many of the sections that do remain are in remarkably good condition. As mentioned above the wall utilises the natural features of the Whin Sill for much of its length. Nowhere is this more in evidence than the spectacular section from Walltown to Sewingshield Crags.

When standing by the wall you cannot help being in awe of its sheer scale and ingenuity not to mention the effort required to have carried out the project in just eight years.

CHEVIOT HILLS

Wandering on the hills in the Northumberland National Park is a truly magical experience. There is always something to see whether it be the wildlife with deer bounding across the moors, adders nestled in the grass or curlews in flight. One of the great pleasures is stumbling across one of the many waterfalls hidden along the course of a hillside burn. The first sign is the distant gurgle of water and as you approach the noise increases until you arrive at a beautiful cascade. I have included a number of these waterfalls (locally called linns) in the book. I also enjoy watching the colours change with the seasons from winter, draped with snow, to spring and summer with vibrant fresh greens and then the splash of autumn colour, vivid reds, oranges and yellows.

KIELDER WATER AND FOREST PARK

Kielder Water is northern Europe's largest man-made lake and the forest is the largest in England. The many miles of forest trails and 27 miles of shoreline make this an extremely popular destination for holidaymakers.

THE COAST

One of the other gems of Northumberland is its coastline. Designated an Area of Outstanding Natural Beauty it stretches some 100 miles in length. There are miles upon miles of unspoilt sandy beaches or waves crashing on rugged, rocky outcrops. Facing east, the coast is a superb location to watch the sunrise. Combine unspoilt coastline with historic castles and spectacular dawn colours and you have a recipe for some stunning views.

TAKING THE PHOTOGRAPHS

I would like to include just a few words about how the photographs in this book were taken. In terms of equipment, I normally use two digital SLR cameras with a collection of lenses including telephoto for picking out distant detail. I also carry a number of filters – graduated filters to balance strong contrast in the light e.g. bright sunlight with dark foreground. The only other filters I use are UV filters to reduce haze and protect the lenses and a polarising filter to saturate colours and reduce glare especially on water.

The photographs in this book are composed of three separate images which are then stitched together using image editing software. I prefer to do this manually rather than use software which automatically creates panoramic images, in this way I can retain full control.

I always use a tripod as much of my work is done in low light conditions requiring long exposure times. Put all of this equipment into a backpack, add a few spare batteries, torch, flask and some waterproofs you end up with a pack weighing in at around thirty pounds, which is fine for a short hop but becomes a bit of a millstone for longer journeys. Some of the walks in the Cheviots for example can involve trips of around 15 miles but you can then add on considerably more miles due to backtracking and excursions trying to get the best vantage point for a view.

During the making of this book I also had to contend with some extreme weather conditions, which presented their own unique challenges. January 2010 had the greatest recorded snowfall in the country for thirty years, which from a landscape photographer's point of view is a mixed blessing. On one hand you have these fantastic snow scenes and on the other you cannot get to them! When you do manage to get within range the walking becomes so much more severe. For example the walk to Coe Crags in Thrunton Wood is a round trip of about 4 miles. From the start the snow was 2 to 3 feet deep. Being the first person there since the snowfall every step was energy sapping. The higher I got the deeper the snow until on the summit ridge between Coe Crags and Long Crag I found myself wading waist deep in powder snow: at one point it took over thirty minutes to cover a hundred yards. There were a number of photographic opportunities available but it was impossible to cover the ground in the circumstances. It must have taken about four hours to cover the distance I would normally cover in ninety minutes.

I never mind the effort involved, often the greater the challenge the greater the reward. I just feel blessed that I live and work in such a beautiful county as Northumberland.

Winter Cheviot
The Cheviots in winter from Thrunton Wood with sunlight highlighting Long Crag, Dunmoor Hill and Cunyan Crags. The Cheviot and Hedgehope are shrouded in cloud. Thrunton Wood offers a fantastic viewpoint over the Cheviots especially from the track along the top of Thrunton Crag.

Hedgehope Grass
Late afternoon sunlight over cloud covered Cheviot and Hedgehope from near the summit of Dunmoor Hill above the village of Linhope in the Breamish Valley. In autumn the grasses take on warm colours from deep reds to bright yellow and orange.

Long Crags

These are the Long Crags in Harthope Valley above the hamlet of Langleeford.
The walk up from the valley offers the opportunity to wander around these
Crags together with Langlee and Housey Crags which give excellent views
across the valley to the Cheviot. The Hill on the left of the photograph is
Blackseat Hill, cut by Hawsen Burn, which separates it from Cold Law.

Thrunton Wood

A view across Thrunton Wood from Long Crag. To the left by the tall tree Windy Gyle can just be seen. Near the centre the long whaleback of the Cheviot leads the eye to Hedghope and just in front of Hedgehope we can see Dunmoor Hill.

Windy Gyle from Coe Crags
Snow-covered trees near the ridge between Coe Crags and Long Crag at Thrunton Wood. In the distance are Mozie Law to the left and slightly higher Windy Gyle. The summit ridges of these hills mark the border between England and Scotland.

Linhope Spout

Linhope Spout is a very well visited waterfall located in the Breamish Valley near the small hamlet of Linhope. Like many of the waterfalls or linns in the Northumberland National Park it hides its delights until the very last moment. Nestled in a very pleasant gorge it is an ideal spot for a picnic and to watch the water tumble down the 18 metre drop. The last time I visited the spot was late in 2009 after severe flooding in Northumberland where I discovered a huge tree trunk laying almost the full length of the waterfall, which I suspect, will remain there for some time to come.

Shillhope Law

Shillhope Law from the Border County Ride, an old cattle drover's track
used for hundreds of years to move cattle between England and Scotland.

Langleeford Hope
Sunlight hitting the small Farmhouse at Langleeford Hope in the Harthope
Valley in the Cheviot Hills within the Northumberland National Park.

Harthope Valley
Dappled sunlight picking out the spectacular autumn colours of the Harthope Valley from the slopes of Hedgehope. The small hamlet of Langleeford can be seen nestling in the valley below Cold Law.

Harthope Linn

Located in the upper reaches of the Harthope Valley a short distance past
Langleeford Hope lies this delightful waterfall on the Harthope Burn.

Broadstruther

This is a remote and delightful spot in the Cheviots, consisting of a small copse of trees and the old shepherd's cottage, which has now been converted into a hunting lodge. It must have been a very lonely existence for the original occupants, particularly in the cold winter months

Long Crag

Long Crag is a very common name in Northumberland for obvious reasons. This particular Long Crag is the one just below the summit of Dunmoor Hill near Linhope in the Breamish Valley. Here the late afternoon light is highlighting the red tinted autumn grass by one of the many small pools found on the top. Beyond the crags by the pool the mist is starting to form over the summit of Hedgehope.

The Schill at Sunset
Fabulous sunset colours over the Schill from the Border Ridge at the head of the College Valley. The Border Ridge is so called because it is the divide between England and Scotland. To the right you can just see the western slopes of the Cheviot dropping into the College Valley.

College Valley Snow
Beautifully wind-sculpted snowdrifts along a stone wall on the slopes of Great Hetha in the College Valley near Hethpool.

College Valley
Looking down the remote College Valley from the slopes of Great Hetha.

Davidson's Linn
A remote waterfall on the Usway Burn found in woodland on the path between Linhope in the Breamish Valley and the Border Ridge. The waterfall is split into two separate falls, this being the larger of the two.

Cheviot sunset from Carter Bar
Late evening light over the Cheviot Hills from the footpath on the hillside to the west of Carter Bar. The Cheviot itself can be seen in the centre just being brushed by the clouds. Carter Bar lies on the border between England and Scotland, a beautiful and remote location offering superb views due to its elevated position. The A68 road from Scotland takes the driver through the beautiful Redesdale Valley, a route that has a long history stretching back many centuries.

Hindhope Linn

This delightful waterfall can be found on the Hindhope Burn a short walk
from the A68 between Otterburn and Jedburgh. The trail is well signposted
and is located near the top of the Forest Drive through Kielder Forest.

Thrunton Wood Sunset
Trees in the deep snow on the ridge between Long Crag and Coe Crags at the south end of Thrunton Wood. The sun can just be seen dropping below the horizon picking out the icicles on the tree. This was taken during the record snowfalls of January 2010. This is a walk I have done many times before but never has it been so energy sapping as on this particular occasion. From the start of the walk the snow was two feet deep and by the end was actually waist deep in places.

Rothbury Sunrise

On the northern side of the village of Rothbury above the Coquet Valley is a series of footpaths that offer superb views across the valley to the Simonside Hills. An easy walk to the top offers superb rewards, as there are also excellent views to the Cheviot Hills in the north. In this photograph taken just before sunrise the village can just be seen behind the cairn.

Simonside Snow

Simonside, lying within the boundary of Northumberland National Park, south of the River Coquet offers superb views across the valley to the Cheviot Hills in the north. Simonside is close to the delightful market town of Rothbury and very popular with walkers. Here it is draped with snow and seen from the path from Lordenshaw to the east. The summit cairn, which can be seen at the end of the path working its way up the hill to the right of the crags, offers a superb vantage point.

Ravens Heugh Crags

Late evening sunlight over Ravens Heugh Crags on the Simonside Hills. The spot offers unrivalled views across Coquetdale. Tosson Hill can be seen on the left sloping down to the valley.

Corby's Crags

Corby's Crags are located conveniently on the B6341 road between Rothbury and Alnwick. There are a number of parking spots along the tops of the crags, which are very popular either for just stopping to take in the views, or for rock climbers seeking access to the crags. Here the late evening sun warms the crags.

Rothbury
Pre dawn light through a line of trees just outside the village of Rothbury.

Thrum Mill

Thrum Mill near Rothbury is located on the banks of the River Coquet and was once a busy flour mill dating back to the seventeenth century. It is believed that the name derives from an area of the river just downstream of this photograph where a natural rock feature narrows the river speeding up the flow of water and creating a thrumming or drumming noise.

Amble Harbour
Looking across the River Coquet to Amble Harbour before dawn.
Amble is a thriving fishing harbour and also has a sizable marina.

Bamburgh Castle Dawn
Soft early morning light over Bamburgh Castle. The castle, built on a basalt outcrop overlooking the North Sea, was restored in 1750. Further restoration took place in the nineteenth century by the first Lord Armstrong.

Dunstanburgh Castle Stones
The south end of Embleton Bay near Dunstanburgh Castle is littered with these impressive basalt boulders, beautiful to look at but treacherous to walk over! Many of the boulders are black and smooth but others are encrusted with barnacles and limpets.

Warkworth Castle
Warkworth Castle taken from the River Coquet near the rowing boat station. The castle, built in the twelfth century is located on high ground at a bend on the river. The castle dominates the beautiful village of Warkworth.

Lindisfarne Castle
The beautiful castle at Lindisfarne is built upon a volcanic outcrop known as Beblowe Craig. The castle was built in the 1550s using stone from the demolished priory. This picture was taken from the public footpath, which skirts around the northern side of the castle.

Farne Islands Sunrise

A great foreground for the rising sun over the Farne Islands. The Farne Islands sit about six miles out to sea and are very popular for boat trips from Seahouses. The islands have much to offer including the famous colonies of puffins and grey seals.

Alnwick Castle Night
The castle just before dawn from the north side.

Plessey Woods
The River Blyth gently running through the Plessey Woods Country Park in autumn.

Bamburgh Castle Rocks
Early evening sunlight over Bamburgh Castle from Harkness Rocks just to the north of the castle.

Bamburgh Castle Grass
Bamburgh Castle with early morning mist seen through grass on the sand dunes.

Lindisfarne Castle Sunrise
A subtle winter sunrise near Lindisfarne Castle. The stakes in the foreground are the remains of the old jetty used to export burnt lime from the Lime Kilns near the castle and to import coal for use in those kilns.

Alnwick Castle Snow
Alnwick Castle and the Lion Bridge reflected in the River Aln. Alnwick Castle was originally built as a medieval fortress in the 1300s and is now the second largest inhabited castle in England after Windsor Castle.

Embleton Bay

Dunstanburgh Castle from Embleton Bay. Amazing sunrise colours over the bay.
The colours only lasted for a few minutes before fading. I remember the surreal
feeling when looking down at the blood red water reflecting the colours in the sky.

Kielder Sunset

Sunset from the Elk picnic site, an elevated location offering superb views over the reservoir.

Kielder Sunset
Last rays of sunlight over rock and grass overlooking Kielder Water.

Kielder Water

One of many small bays to be found around the shore of Kielder Water. The reservoir has footpaths around its entire 27-mile perimeter offering the opportunity to fully explore and uncover its many delights.

Kielder Water

Kielder Water about an hour after sunset. This photograph was taken near the Tower Knowe viewpoint to the south east of the reservoir. A really serene place to sit and watch the sunset. If ever there was a recipe for peace and tranquillity I am sure that water, trees, hills and sky would be some of the main ingredients.

Beadnell Harbour
Beadnell Harbour just before dawn. The harbour is located to the north
end of the delightful Beadnell Bay, which is just over 2 miles in length.

Seaton Sluice Dawn
Seaton Sluice is the southernmost village on the Northumberland coast. In the eighteenth century it was the port for the largest bottle-making factory in England. Here the waves can be seen crashing against the pier, which protects the mouth of the harbour.

Alnmouth Sunrise

Sunrise from Church Hill, Alnmouth. The village of Alnmouth as the name suggests is located at the mouth of the River Aln. Alnmouth is very popular with holidaymakers and day trippers, attracted by the superb beaches and walking. The cross on Church Hill is a fairly recent one. Church Hill is so called because it used to be the location of the Alnmouth church, which was cut off from the village in 1806 by a huge storm, which actually altered the course of the River Aln.

Farne Island Sunrise
Facing east, the Northumberland coast is perfect for watching the sunrise. I was lucky enough to be on the beach near Bamburgh looking out to the Farne Islands and was blessed with this magnificent display of colour. The colour only lasted for a few minutes and then quickly faded back to grey.

Lindisfarne Boat

A small boat settled on the mud in the harbour on the Holy Island of Lindisfarne with the castle in the background. I think the name of the boat sums up the scene, Pax being Latin for peace. In fact the whole of Lindisfarne itself is an amazingly tranquil place. As soon as you cross the causeway, which links the island to the mainland twice a day, you can understand why St Aidan built the first monastery here in 635AD.

Steel Rigg Sunrise
Sunrise over Peel Crags on Hadrian's Wall above Crag Lough with Hotbank Crags rising in the distance

Hadrian's Wall from Cuddy's Crag
Sunrise from Cuddy's Crag on Hadrian's Wall near Housesteads Roman Fort. The Romans made good use of the Whin Sill, a natural feature created some 400 million years ago due to the collision of two continental plates. The course of the wall can be seen following the line of this incredible natural divide.

103

Sycamore Gap

This must be one of the most photographed locations on Hadrian's Wall. The sycamore tree, by all accounts, is lucky to be standing today as it was supposedly scheduled to be cut down when it was a mere sapling but for some reason escaped. The location was made more famous after its inclusion in the film *Robin Hood Prince of Thieves*.

Hadrian's Wall from Hotbank Crags
The wall looking to the east from near Hotbank. The distinctive shape of Sewingshields Crags can be seen in the distance with Broomlee Lough.

Winshield Crags

Winshield Crags on Hadrian's Wall seen from Peel Crags above Crag Lough. There is a car park by the trees just in front of the crags giving easy access to both Winshield Crags and Steel Rigg and Peel Crags.

Sewingshields Crags

This is a telephoto image taken from near Cuddy's Crags on Hadrians Wall. I had intended to capture a sunset in the west but as so often happens it was quite uninspiring. However, when I turned around I spotted the incredible light and the last rays of sunlight picking out the crags at Sewingshields and Queens Crag to the left.

Steel Rigg
The heavy snowfalls of early 2010 provided a unique opportuni
to take this image from Steel Rigg on Hadrian's Wall.